This Cleaning Journal Belongs to

_____
_____

Spring Clean

Room: Living Room

- ☐ Clean Cabinets
- ☐ Clean Doors & Windows
- ☐ Clean Floors/Rugs
- ☐ Clean Furniture
- ☐ Clean Appliances
- ☐ Clean Curtains/Blinds/Linen

Date & Time of Spring Clean:
_____
_____

Cleaning Items Needed:
_____
_____
_____
_____
_____

Cabinet/Drawers Inventory
_____
_____
_____
_____
_____

I Need to Dust:
_____
_____
_____

I Need to Wash:
_____
_____
_____

Other Cleaning Tasks:
_____
_____

Other Tidying/Organising Tasks
_____
_____

Room Completed ☐

Spring Clean

Room: Dining Room

- [ ] Clean Cabinets
- [ ] Clean Doors & Windows
- [ ] Clean Floors/Rugs
- [ ] Clean Furniture
- [ ] Clean Appliances
- [ ] Clean Curtains/Blinds/Linen

Date & Time of Spring Clean:

_____
_____

Cleaning Items Needed:

_____
_____
_____
_____
_____
_____

Cabinet/Drawers Inventory

_____
_____
_____
_____
_____
_____

I Need to Dust:

_____
_____

I Need to Wash:

_____
_____

Other Cleaning Tasks:

_____
_____

Other Tidying/Organising Tasks

_____
_____

Room Completed [ ]

Spring Clean

Room: Kitchen

Date & Time of Spring Clean:
_____
_____

- ☐ Clean Cabinets

Cleaning Items Needed:
_____
_____
_____
_____
_____
_____

- ☐ Clean Doors & Windows

- ☐ Clean Floors/Rugs

Cabinet/Drawers Inventory
_____
_____

- ☐ Clean Furniture

_____
_____

- ☐ Clean Appliances

_____
_____

- ☐ Clean Curtains/Blinds/Linen

I Need to Dust:
_____
_____
_____

I Need to Wash:
_____
_____
_____

Other Cleaning Tasks:
_____
_____

Other Tidying/Organising Tasks
_____
_____

Room Completed ☐

Spring Clean

Room:
Bathroom #1

- [ ] Clean Cabinets
- [ ] Clean Doors & Windows
- [ ] Clean Floors/Rugs
- [ ] Clean Furniture
- [ ] Clean Appliances
- [ ] Clean Curtains/Blinds/Linen

Date & Time of Spring Clean:
_____
_____

Cleaning Items Needed:
_____
_____
_____
_____
_____
_____
_____

Cabinet/Drawers Inventory
_____
_____
_____
_____
_____
_____
_____
_____
_____

I Need to Dust:
_____
_____
_____

I Need to Wash:
_____
_____
_____

Other Cleaning Tasks:
_____
_____

Other Tidying/Organising Tasks
_____
_____

Room Completed [ ]

Spring Clean

Room:
Bathroom #2

Date & Time of Spring Clean:
_____
_____

- [ ] Clean Cabinets
- [ ] Clean Doors & Windows
- [ ] Clean Floors/Rugs
- [ ] Clean Furniture
- [ ] Clean Appliances
- [ ] Clean Curtains/Blinds/Linen

Cleaning Items Needed:
_____
_____
_____
_____
_____
_____

Cabinet/Drawers Inventory
_____
_____
_____
_____
_____
_____
_____

I Need to Dust:
_____
_____

I Need to Wash:
_____
_____

Other Cleaning Tasks:
_____
_____

Other Tidying/Organising Tasks
_____
_____

Room Completed [ ]

Spring Clean

Room:
Bathroom #3

- [ ] Clean Cabinets
- [ ] Clean Doors & Windows
- [ ] Clean Floors/Rugs
- [ ] Clean Furniture
- [ ] Clean Appliances
- [ ] Clean Curtains/Blinds/Linen

Date & Time of Spring Clean:
_____
_____

Cleaning Items Needed:
_____
_____
_____
_____
_____
_____
_____

Cabinet/Drawers Inventory
_____
_____
_____
_____
_____
_____
_____
_____

I Need to Dust:
_____
_____
_____

I Need to Wash:
_____
_____

Other Cleaning Tasks:
_____
_____

Other Tidying/Organising Tasks
_____
_____

Room Completed [ ]

Spring Clean

Room: Laundry Room

- ☐ Clean Cabinets
- ☐ Clean Doors & Windows
- ☐ Clean Floors/Rugs
- ☐ Clean Furniture
- ☐ Clean Appliances
- ☐ Clean Curtains/Blinds/Linen

Date & Time of Spring Clean:

_____

_____

Cleaning Items Needed:

_____

_____

_____

_____

_____

_____

Cabinet/Drawers Inventory

_____

_____

_____

_____

_____

_____

I Need to Dust:

_____

_____

_____

I Need to Wash:

_____

_____

_____

Other Cleaning Tasks:

_____

_____

Other Tidying/Organising Tasks

_____

_____

Room Completed ☐

Spring Clean

Room:
Hallway/Corridor

Date & Time of Spring Clean:
_____
_____

- ☐ Clean Cabinets

Cleaning Items Needed:
_____
_____

- ☐ Clean Doors & Windows

_____
_____
_____
_____

- ☐ Clean Floors/Rugs

_____
_____

Cabinet/Drawers Inventory

- ☐ Clean Furniture

_____
_____

- ☐ Clean Appliances

_____
_____
_____

- ☐ Clean Curtains/Blinds/Linen

_____

I Need to Dust: I Need to Wash:
_____   _____
_____   _____
_____   _____

Other Cleaning Tasks:
_____
_____

Other Tidying/Organising Tasks
_____
_____

Room Completed ☐

Spring Clean

Room: Porch/Mud Room

Date & Time of Spring Clean:

- [ ] Clean Cabinets
- [ ] Clean Doors & Windows
- [ ] Clean Floors/Rugs
- [ ] Clean Furniture
- [ ] Clean Appliances
- [ ] Clean Curtains/Blinds/Linen

Cleaning Items Needed:

Cabinet/Drawers Inventory

I Need to Dust:

I Need to Wash:

Other Cleaning Tasks:

Other Tidying/Organising Tasks

Room Completed [ ]

Spring Clean

Room:
Bedroom #1

Date & Time of Spring Clean:
_____
_____

- [ ] Clean Cabinets

Cleaning Items Needed:
_____
_____
_____
_____
_____
_____

- [ ] Clean Doors & Windows

- [ ] Clean Floors/Rugs

Cabinet/Drawers Inventory
_____
_____
_____
_____
_____
_____
_____
_____

- [ ] Clean Furniture

- [ ] Clean Appliances

- [ ] Clean Curtains/Blinds/Linen

I Need to Dust:
_____
_____

I Need to Wash:
_____
_____

Other Cleaning Tasks:
_____
_____

Other Tidying/Organising Tasks
_____
_____

Room Completed [ ]

Spring Clean

Room: Bedroom #2

- [ ] Clean Cabinets
- [ ] Clean Doors & Windows
- [ ] Clean Floors/Rugs
- [ ] Clean Furniture
- [ ] Clean Appliances
- [ ] Clean Curtains/Blinds/Linen

Date & Time of Spring Clean:

Cleaning Items Needed:

Cabinet/Drawers Inventory

I Need to Dust:

I Need to Wash:

Other Cleaning Tasks:

Other Tidying/Organising Tasks

Room Completed [ ]

Spring Clean

Room: Bedroom #3

- ☐ Clean Cabinets
- ☐ Clean Doors & Windows
- ☐ Clean Floors/Rugs
- ☐ Clean Furniture
- ☐ Clean Appliances
- ☐ Clean Curtains/Blinds/Linen

Date & Time of Spring Clean:

_____
_____

Cleaning Items Needed:

_____
_____
_____
_____
_____
_____

Cabinet/Drawers Inventory

_____
_____
_____
_____
_____
_____

I Need to Dust:

_____
_____

I Need to Wash:

_____
_____

Other Cleaning Tasks:

_____
_____

Other Tidying/Organising Tasks

_____
_____

Room Completed ☐

Spring Clean

Room:
Bedroom #4

- [ ] Clean Cabinets
- [ ] Clean Doors & Windows
- [ ] Clean Floors/Rugs
- [ ] Clean Furniture
- [ ] Clean Appliances
- [ ] Clean Curtains/Blinds/Linen

Date & Time of Spring Clean:

_____

Cleaning Items Needed:

_____
_____
_____
_____
_____

Cabinet/Drawers Inventory

_____
_____
_____
_____
_____

I Need to Dust:

_____
_____

I Need to Wash:

_____
_____

Other Cleaning Tasks:

_____
_____

Other Tidying/Organising Tasks

_____
_____

Room Completed [ ]

Spring Clean

Room: Bedroom #5

- [ ] Clean Cabinets
- [ ] Clean Doors & Windows
- [ ] Clean Floors/Rugs
- [ ] Clean Furniture
- [ ] Clean Appliances
- [ ] Clean Curtains/Blinds/Linen

Date & Time of Spring Clean:

_____
_____

Cleaning Items Needed:

_____
_____
_____
_____
_____
_____
_____

Cabinet/Drawers Inventory

_____
_____
_____
_____
_____
_____
_____

I Need to Dust:

_____
_____

I Need to Wash:

_____
_____

Other Cleaning Tasks:

_____
_____

Other Tidying/Organising Tasks

_____
_____

Room Completed [ ]

Spring Clean

Room: Office

- [ ] Clean Cabinets
- [ ] Clean Doors & Windows
- [ ] Clean Floors/Rugs
- [ ] Clean Furniture
- [ ] Clean Appliances
- [ ] Clean Curtains/Blinds/Linen

Date & Time of Spring Clean:
_____

Cleaning Items Needed:
_____
_____
_____
_____
_____

Cabinet/Drawers Inventory
_____
_____
_____
_____
_____
_____

I Need to Dust:
_____
_____
_____

I Need to Wash:
_____
_____
_____

Other Cleaning Tasks:
_____
_____

Other Tidying/Organising Tasks
_____
_____

Room Completed [ ]

Spring Clean

Room: Games Room

- ☐ Clean Cabinets
- ☐ Clean Doors & Windows
- ☐ Clean Floors/Rugs
- ☐ Clean Furniture
- ☐ Clean Appliances
- ☐ Clean Curtains/Blinds/Linen

Date & Time of Spring Clean:
_____
_____

Cleaning Items Needed:
_____
_____
_____
_____
_____
_____

Cabinet/Drawers Inventory
_____
_____
_____
_____
_____
_____

I Need to Dust:
_____
_____

I Need to Wash:
_____
_____

Other Cleaning Tasks:
_____
_____

Other Tidying/Organising Tasks
_____
_____

Room Completed ☐

Spring Clean

Room: Basement

- ☐ Clean Cabinets
- ☐ Clean Doors & Windows
- ☐ Clean Floors/Rugs
- ☐ Clean Furniture
- ☐ Clean Appliances
- ☐ Clean Curtains/Blinds/Linen

Date & Time of Spring Clean:

Cleaning Items Needed:

Cabinet/Drawers Inventory

I Need to Dust:

I Need to Wash:

Other Cleaning Tasks:

Other Tidying/Organising Tasks

Room Completed ☐

Spring Clean

Room: Garage

- [ ] Clean Cabinets
- [ ] Clean Doors & Windows
- [ ] Clean Floors/Rugs
- [ ] Clean Furniture
- [ ] Clean Appliances
- [ ] Clean Curtains/Blinds/Linen

Date & Time of Spring Clean:
_____
_____

Cleaning Items Needed:
_____
_____
_____
_____
_____
_____

Cabinet/Drawers Inventory
_____
_____
_____
_____
_____
_____
_____

I Need to Dust:
_____
_____
_____

I Need to Wash:
_____
_____
_____

Other Cleaning Tasks:
_____
_____

Other Tidying/Organising Tasks
_____
_____

Room Completed [ ]

Spring Clean

Room:
Other _____

Date & Time of Spring Clean:
_____
_____

Cleaning Items Needed:
_____
_____
_____
_____
_____
_____

- [ ] Clean Cabinets
- [ ] Clean Doors & Windows
- [ ] Clean Floors/Rugs
- [ ] Clean Furniture
- [ ] Clean Appliances
- [ ] Clean Curtains/Blinds/Linen

Cabinet/Drawers Inventory
_____
_____
_____
_____
_____
_____

I Need to Dust:
_____
_____
_____

I Need to Wash:
_____
_____

Other Cleaning Tasks:
_____
_____

Other Tidying/Organising Tasks
_____
_____

Room Completed [ ]

Spring Clean

Room:
Other _____

Date & Time of Spring Clean:
_____
_____

- [ ] Clean Cabinets

Cleaning Items Needed:
_____
_____
_____
_____
_____

- [ ] Clean Doors & Windows

- [ ] Clean Floors/Rugs

Cabinet/Drawers Inventory
_____
_____
_____
_____
_____
_____

- [ ] Clean Furniture

- [ ] Clean Appliances

- [ ] Clean Curtains/Blinds/Linen

I Need to Dust:
_____
_____
_____

I Need to Wash:
_____
_____
_____

Other Cleaning Tasks:
_____
_____

Other Tidying/Organising Tasks
_____
_____

Room Completed [ ]

Spring Clean

Room: Other _____

- ☐ Clean Cabinets
- ☐ Clean Doors & Windows
- ☐ Clean Floors/Rugs
- ☐ Clean Furniture
- ☐ Clean Appliances
- ☐ Clean Curtains/Blinds/Linen

Date & Time of Spring Clean:
_____
_____

Cleaning Items Needed:
_____
_____
_____
_____
_____
_____

Cabinet/Drawers Inventory
_____
_____
_____
_____
_____
_____

I Need to Dust:
_____
_____
_____

I Need to Wash:
_____
_____

Other Cleaning Tasks:
_____
_____

Other Tidying/Organising Tasks
_____
_____

Room Completed ☐

Spring Clean

Room:
Other _____

Date & Time of Spring Clean:
_____
_____

- [ ] Clean Cabinets

Cleaning Items Needed:
_____
_____
_____
_____
_____

- [ ] Clean Doors & Windows

_____
_____
_____

- [ ] Clean Floors/Rugs

Cabinet/Drawers Inventory
_____
_____

- [ ] Clean Furniture

_____
_____
_____
_____

- [ ] Clean Appliances

_____
_____
_____

- [ ] Clean Curtains/Blinds/Linen

I Need to Dust: I Need to Wash:
_____   _____
_____   _____
_____   _____

Other Cleaning Tasks:
_____
_____

Other Tidying/Organising Tasks
_____
_____

oom Completed [ ]

Spring Clean

Room:
Other _____

- ☐ Clean Cabinets
- ☐ Clean Doors & Windows
- ☐ Clean Floors/Rugs
- ☐ Clean Furniture
- ☐ Clean Appliances
- ☐ Clean Curtains/Blinds/Linen

Date & Time of Spring Clean:
_____
_____

Cleaning Items Needed:
_____
_____
_____
_____
_____
_____

Cabinet/Drawers Inventory
_____
_____
_____
_____
_____
_____
_____

I Need to Dust:
_____
_____
_____

I Need to Wash:
_____
_____

Other Cleaning Tasks:
_____
_____

Other Tidying/Organising Tasks
_____
_____

Room Completed ☐

Spring Clean

Room: Other _____

- [ ] Clean Cabinets
- [ ] Clean Doors & Windows
- [ ] Clean Floors/Rugs
- [ ] Clean Furniture
- [ ] Clean Appliances
- [ ] Clean Curtains/Blinds/Linen

Date & Time of Spring Clean:
_____
_____

Cleaning Items Needed:
_____
_____
_____
_____
_____
_____

Cabinet/Drawers Inventory
_____
_____
_____
_____
_____
_____

I Need to Dust:
_____
_____
_____

I Need to Wash:
_____
_____
_____

Other Cleaning Tasks:
_____
_____

Other Tidying/Organising Tasks
_____
_____

Room Completed [ ]

Spring Clean

Garden

Date & Time of Spring Clean:

- ☐ Sweep Pathways & Patios
- ☐ Clear Debris & Leaves
- ☐ Clean Outdoor Furniture
- ☐ Hose Down Driveway
- ☐ Plant Spring Flowers
- ☐ Clean and Tidy Shed/s

Cleaning Items Needed:

Important Gardening Tasks

Outdoor Maintenance Tasks:

I Need to Wash:

Other Outdoor Cleaning Tasks:

Other Tidying/Organising Tasks

Completed ☐

Weekly Clean

Monday

Tuesday

Wednesday

Thursday

Friday

Saturday & Sunday

Notes

Weekly Clean

Monday

- [ ]
- [ ]
- [ ]
- [ ]
- [ ]
- [ ]

Tuesday

- [ ]
- [ ]
- [ ]
- [ ]
- [ ]
- [ ]

Wednesday

- [ ]
- [ ]
- [ ]
- [ ]
- [ ]
- [ ]

Thursday

- [ ]
- [ ]
- [ ]
- [ ]
- [ ]
- [ ]

Friday

- [ ]
- [ ]
- [ ]
- [ ]
- [ ]
- [ ]

Saturday & Sunday

- [ ]
- [ ]
- [ ]
- [ ]
- [ ]
- [ ]

Notes

_____
_____
_____

Weekly Clean

Monday
- [ ]
- [ ]
- [ ]
- [ ]
- [ ]
- [ ]

Tuesday
- [ ]
- [ ]
- [ ]
- [ ]
- [ ]
- [ ]

Wednesday
- [ ]
- [ ]
- [ ]
- [ ]
- [ ]
- [ ]

Thursday
- [ ]
- [ ]
- [ ]
- [ ]
- [ ]
- [ ]

Friday
- [ ]
- [ ]
- [ ]
- [ ]
- [ ]
- [ ]

Saturday & Sunday
- [ ]
- [ ]
- [ ]
- [ ]
- [ ]
- [ ]

Notes

Weekly Clean

Monday
Tuesday
Wednesday
Thursday
Friday
Saturday & Sunday

Notes

Weekly Clean

Monday

Tuesday

Wednesday

Thursday

Friday

Saturday & Sunday

Notes

Weekly Clean

Monday
- [ ]
- [ ]
- [ ]
- [ ]
- [ ]
- [ ]

Tuesday
- [ ]
- [ ]
- [ ]
- [ ]
- [ ]
- [ ]

Wednesday
- [ ]
- [ ]
- [ ]
- [ ]
- [ ]
- [ ]

Thursday
- [ ]
- [ ]
- [ ]
- [ ]
- [ ]
- [ ]

Friday
- [ ]
- [ ]
- [ ]
- [ ]
- [ ]
- [ ]

Saturday & Sunday
- [ ]
- [ ]
- [ ]
- [ ]
- [ ]
- [ ]

Notes
_____
_____
_____
_____

Weekly Clean

Monday

- [ ]
- [ ]
- [ ]
- [ ]
- [ ]
- [ ]

Tuesday

- [ ]
- [ ]
- [ ]
- [ ]
- [ ]
- [ ]

Wednesday

- [ ]
- [ ]
- [ ]
- [ ]
- [ ]
- [ ]

Thursday

- [ ]
- [ ]
- [ ]
- [ ]
- [ ]
- [ ]

Friday

- [ ]
- [ ]
- [ ]
- [ ]
- [ ]
- [ ]

Saturday & Sunday

- [ ]
- [ ]
- [ ]
- [ ]
- [ ]
- [ ]

Notes

Weekly Clean

Monday
- [ ]
- [ ]
- [ ]
- [ ]
- [ ]
- [ ]

Tuesday
- [ ]
- [ ]
- [ ]
- [ ]
- [ ]
- [ ]

Wednesday
- [ ]
- [ ]
- [ ]
- [ ]
- [ ]
- [ ]

Thursday
- [ ]
- [ ]
- [ ]
- [ ]
- [ ]
- [ ]

Friday
- [ ]
- [ ]
- [ ]
- [ ]
- [ ]
- [ ]

Saturday & Sunday
- [ ]
- [ ]
- [ ]
- [ ]
- [ ]
- [ ]

Notes

Weekly Clean

Monday
- [ ]
- [ ]
- [ ]
- [ ]
- [ ]
- [ ]

Tuesday
- [ ]
- [ ]
- [ ]
- [ ]
- [ ]
- [ ]

Wednesday
- [ ]
- [ ]
- [ ]
- [ ]
- [ ]
- [ ]

Thursday
- [ ]
- [ ]
- [ ]
- [ ]
- [ ]
- [ ]

Friday
- [ ]
- [ ]
- [ ]
- [ ]
- [ ]
- [ ]

Saturday & Sunday
- [ ]
- [ ]
- [ ]
- [ ]
- [ ]
- [ ]

Notes
_____
_____
_____
_____

Weekly Clean

Monday
- [ ]
- [ ]
- [ ]
- [ ]
- [ ]
- [ ]

Tuesday
- [ ]
- [ ]
- [ ]
- [ ]
- [ ]
- [ ]

Wednesday
- [ ]
- [ ]
- [ ]
- [ ]
- [ ]
- [ ]

Thursday
- [ ]
- [ ]
- [ ]
- [ ]
- [ ]
- [ ]

Friday
- [ ]
- [ ]
- [ ]
- [ ]
- [ ]
- [ ]

Saturday & Sunday
- [ ]
- [ ]
- [ ]
- [ ]
- [ ]
- [ ]

Notes
_____
_____
_____

Weekly Clean

Monday
- [ ]
- [ ]
- [ ]
- [ ]
- [ ]
- [ ]

Tuesday
- [ ]
- [ ]
- [ ]
- [ ]
- [ ]
- [ ]

Wednesday
- [ ]
- [ ]
- [ ]
- [ ]
- [ ]
- [ ]

Thursday
- [ ]
- [ ]
- [ ]
- [ ]
- [ ]
- [ ]

Friday
- [ ]
- [ ]
- [ ]
- [ ]
- [ ]
- [ ]

Saturday & Sunday
- [ ]
- [ ]
- [ ]
- [ ]
- [ ]
- [ ]

Notes

_____
_____
_____
_____

Weekly Clean

Monday
- [ ]
- [ ]
- [ ]
- [ ]
- [ ]
- [ ]

Tuesday
- [ ]
- [ ]
- [ ]
- [ ]
- [ ]
- [ ]

Wednesday
- [ ]
- [ ]
- [ ]
- [ ]
- [ ]
- [ ]

Thursday
- [ ]
- [ ]
- [ ]
- [ ]
- [ ]
- [ ]

Friday
- [ ]
- [ ]
- [ ]
- [ ]
- [ ]
- [ ]

Saturday & Sunday
- [ ]
- [ ]
- [ ]
- [ ]
- [ ]
- [ ]

Notes

_____
_____
_____
_____

Weekly Clean

Monday

Tuesday

Wednesday

Thursday

Friday

Saturday & Sunday

Notes

Weekly Clean

Monday

Tuesday

Wednesday

Thursday

Friday

Saturday & Sunday

Notes

Weekly Clean

Monday

Tuesday

Wednesday

Thursday

Friday

Saturday & Sunday

Notes

Weekly Clean

Monday
- [ ]
- [ ]
- [ ]
- [ ]
- [ ]
- [ ]

Tuesday
- [ ]
- [ ]
- [ ]
- [ ]
- [ ]
- [ ]

Wednesday
- [ ]
- [ ]
- [ ]
- [ ]
- [ ]
- [ ]

Thursday
- [ ]
- [ ]
- [ ]
- [ ]
- [ ]
- [ ]

Friday
- [ ]
- [ ]
- [ ]
- [ ]
- [ ]
- [ ]

Saturday & Sunday
- [ ]
- [ ]
- [ ]
- [ ]
- [ ]
- [ ]

Notes

Weekly Clean

Monday
- [ ]
- [ ]
- [ ]
- [ ]
- [ ]
- [ ]

Tuesday
- [ ]
- [ ]
- [ ]
- [ ]
- [ ]
- [ ]

Wednesday
- [ ]
- [ ]
- [ ]
- [ ]
- [ ]
- [ ]

Thursday
- [ ]
- [ ]
- [ ]
- [ ]
- [ ]
- [ ]

Friday
- [ ]
- [ ]
- [ ]
- [ ]
- [ ]
- [ ]

Saturday & Sunday
- [ ]
- [ ]
- [ ]
- [ ]
- [ ]
- [ ]

Notes

Weekly Clean

Monday

- [ ]
- [ ]
- [ ]
- [ ]
- [ ]
- [ ]

Tuesday

- [ ]
- [ ]
- [ ]
- [ ]
- [ ]
- [ ]

Wednesday

- [ ]
- [ ]
- [ ]
- [ ]
- [ ]
- [ ]

Thursday

- [ ]
- [ ]
- [ ]
- [ ]
- [ ]
- [ ]

Friday

- [ ]
- [ ]
- [ ]
- [ ]
- [ ]
- [ ]

Saturday & Sunday

- [ ]
- [ ]
- [ ]
- [ ]
- [ ]
- [ ]

Notes

_____
_____
_____
_____

Weekly Clean

Monday	Tuesday	Wednesday
☐	☐	☐
☐	☐	☐
☐	☐	☐
☐	☐	☐
☐	☐	☐
☐	☐	☐

Thursday	Friday	Saturday & Sunday
☐	☐	☐
☐	☐	☐
☐	☐	☐
☐	☐	☐
☐	☐	☐
☐	☐	☐

Notes

Weekly Clean

Monday

Tuesday

Wednesday

Thursday

Friday

Saturday & Sunday

Notes

Weekly Clean

Monday

Tuesday

Wednesday

Thursday

Friday

Saturday & Sunday

Notes

Weekly Clean

Monday

- [ ]
- [ ]
- [ ]
- [ ]
- [ ]
- [ ]

Tuesday

- [ ]
- [ ]
- [ ]
- [ ]
- [ ]
- [ ]

Wednesday

- [ ]
- [ ]
- [ ]
- [ ]
- [ ]
- [ ]

Thursday

- [ ]
- [ ]
- [ ]
- [ ]
- [ ]
- [ ]

Friday

- [ ]
- [ ]
- [ ]
- [ ]
- [ ]
- [ ]

Saturday & Sunday

- [ ]
- [ ]
- [ ]
- [ ]
- [ ]
- [ ]

Notes

_____
_____
_____

Weekly Clean

Monday

- [ ]
- [ ]
- [ ]
- [ ]
- [ ]
- [ ]

Tuesday

- [ ]
- [ ]
- [ ]
- [ ]
- [ ]
- [ ]

Wednesday

- [ ]
- [ ]
- [ ]
- [ ]
- [ ]
- [ ]

Thursday

- [ ]
- [ ]
- [ ]
- [ ]
- [ ]
- [ ]

Friday

- [ ]
- [ ]
- [ ]
- [ ]
- [ ]
- [ ]

Saturday & Sunday

- [ ]
- [ ]
- [ ]
- [ ]
- [ ]
- [ ]

Notes

_____
_____
_____

Weekly Clean

Monday
- [ ]
- [ ]
- [ ]
- [ ]
- [ ]
- [ ]

Tuesday
- [ ]
- [ ]
- [ ]
- [ ]
- [ ]
- [ ]

Wednesday
- [ ]
- [ ]
- [ ]
- [ ]
- [ ]
- [ ]

Thursday
- [ ]
- [ ]
- [ ]
- [ ]
- [ ]
- [ ]

Friday
- [ ]
- [ ]
- [ ]
- [ ]
- [ ]
- [ ]

Saturday & Sunday
- [ ]
- [ ]
- [ ]
- [ ]
- [ ]
- [ ]

Notes

_____
_____
_____
_____

Weekly Clean

Monday

Tuesday

Wednesday

Thursday

Friday

Saturday & Sunday

Notes

Weekly Clean

Monday
- [ ]
- [ ]
- [ ]
- [ ]
- [ ]
- [ ]

Tuesday
- [ ]
- [ ]
- [ ]
- [ ]
- [ ]
- [ ]

Wednesday
- [ ]
- [ ]
- [ ]
- [ ]
- [ ]
- [ ]

Thursday
- [ ]
- [ ]
- [ ]
- [ ]
- [ ]
- [ ]

Friday
- [ ]
- [ ]
- [ ]
- [ ]
- [ ]
- [ ]

Saturday & Sunday
- [ ]
- [ ]
- [ ]
- [ ]
- [ ]
- [ ]

Notes

_____
_____
_____
_____

Weekly Clean

Monday

- [ ]
- [ ]
- [ ]
- [ ]
- [ ]
- [ ]

Tuesday

- [ ]
- [ ]
- [ ]
- [ ]
- [ ]
- [ ]

Wednesday

- [ ]
- [ ]
- [ ]
- [ ]
- [ ]
- [ ]

Thursday

- [ ]
- [ ]
- [ ]
- [ ]
- [ ]
- [ ]

Friday

- [ ]
- [ ]
- [ ]
- [ ]
- [ ]
- [ ]

Saturday & Sunday

- [ ]
- [ ]
- [ ]
- [ ]
- [ ]
- [ ]

Notes

Weekly Clean

Monday

- [ ]
- [ ]
- [ ]
- [ ]
- [ ]
- [ ]

Tuesday

- [ ]
- [ ]
- [ ]
- [ ]
- [ ]
- [ ]

Wednesday

- [ ]
- [ ]
- [ ]
- [ ]
- [ ]
- [ ]

Thursday

- [ ]
- [ ]
- [ ]
- [ ]
- [ ]
- [ ]

Friday

- [ ]
- [ ]
- [ ]
- [ ]
- [ ]
- [ ]

Saturday & Sunday

- [ ]
- [ ]
- [ ]
- [ ]
- [ ]
- [ ]

Notes

_____
_____
_____
_____

Weekly Clean

Monday

Tuesday

Wednesday

Thursday

Friday

Saturday & Sunday

Notes

Weekly Clean

Monday
- [ ]
- [ ]
- [ ]
- [ ]
- [ ]
- [ ]

Tuesday
- [ ]
- [ ]
- [ ]
- [ ]
- [ ]
- [ ]

Wednesday
- [ ]
- [ ]
- [ ]
- [ ]
- [ ]
- [ ]

Thursday
- [ ]
- [ ]
- [ ]
- [ ]
- [ ]
- [ ]

Friday
- [ ]
- [ ]
- [ ]
- [ ]
- [ ]
- [ ]

Saturday & Sunday
- [ ]
- [ ]
- [ ]
- [ ]
- [ ]
- [ ]

Notes

Weekly Clean

Monday
- [ ]
- [ ]
- [ ]
- [ ]
- [ ]
- [ ]

Tuesday
- [ ]
- [ ]
- [ ]
- [ ]
- [ ]
- [ ]

Wednesday
- [ ]
- [ ]
- [ ]
- [ ]
- [ ]
- [ ]

Thursday
- [ ]
- [ ]
- [ ]
- [ ]
- [ ]
- [ ]

Friday
- [ ]
- [ ]
- [ ]
- [ ]
- [ ]
- [ ]

Saturday & Sunday
- [ ]
- [ ]
- [ ]
- [ ]
- [ ]
- [ ]

Notes

_____
_____
_____
_____

Weekly Clean

Monday
- [ ]
- [ ]
- [ ]
- [ ]
- [ ]
- [ ]

Tuesday
- [ ]
- [ ]
- [ ]
- [ ]
- [ ]
- [ ]

Wednesday
- [ ]
- [ ]
- [ ]
- [ ]
- [ ]
- [ ]

Thursday
- [ ]
- [ ]
- [ ]
- [ ]
- [ ]
- [ ]

Friday
- [ ]
- [ ]
- [ ]
- [ ]
- [ ]
- [ ]

Saturday & Sunday
- [ ]
- [ ]
- [ ]
- [ ]
- [ ]
- [ ]

Notes
_____
_____
_____

Weekly Clean

Monday

- [ ]
- [ ]
- [ ]
- [ ]
- [ ]
- [ ]

Tuesday

- [ ]
- [ ]
- [ ]
- [ ]
- [ ]
- [ ]

Wednesday

- [ ]
- [ ]
- [ ]
- [ ]
- [ ]
- [ ]

Thursday

- [ ]
- [ ]
- [ ]
- [ ]
- [ ]
- [ ]

Friday

- [ ]
- [ ]
- [ ]
- [ ]
- [ ]
- [ ]

Saturday & Sunday

- [ ]
- [ ]
- [ ]
- [ ]
- [ ]
- [ ]

Notes

_____
_____
_____

Weekly Clean

Monday

- [ ]
- [ ]
- [ ]
- [ ]
- [ ]
- [ ]

Tuesday

- [ ]
- [ ]
- [ ]
- [ ]
- [ ]
- [ ]

Wednesday

- [ ]
- [ ]
- [ ]
- [ ]
- [ ]
- [ ]

Thursday

- [ ]
- [ ]
- [ ]
- [ ]
- [ ]
- [ ]

Friday

- [ ]
- [ ]
- [ ]
- [ ]
- [ ]
- [ ]

Saturday & Sunday

- [ ]
- [ ]
- [ ]
- [ ]
- [ ]
- [ ]

Notes

Weekly Clean

Monday
- [ ]
- [ ]
- [ ]
- [ ]
- [ ]
- [ ]

Tuesday
- [ ]
- [ ]
- [ ]
- [ ]
- [ ]
- [ ]

Wednesday
- [ ]
- [ ]
- [ ]
- [ ]
- [ ]
- [ ]

Thursday
- [ ]
- [ ]
- [ ]
- [ ]
- [ ]
- [ ]

Friday
- [ ]
- [ ]
- [ ]
- [ ]
- [ ]
- [ ]

Saturday & Sunday
- [ ]
- [ ]
- [ ]
- [ ]
- [ ]
- [ ]

Notes
_____
_____
_____
_____

Weekly Clean

Monday

Tuesday

Wednesday

Thursday

Friday

Saturday & Sunday

Notes

Weekly Clean

Monday

- [ ]
- [ ]
- [ ]
- [ ]
- [ ]
- [ ]

Tuesday

- [ ]
- [ ]
- [ ]
- [ ]
- [ ]
- [ ]

Wednesday

- [ ]
- [ ]
- [ ]
- [ ]
- [ ]
- [ ]

Thursday

- [ ]
- [ ]
- [ ]
- [ ]
- [ ]
- [ ]

Friday

- [ ]
- [ ]
- [ ]
- [ ]
- [ ]
- [ ]

Saturday & Sunday

- [ ]
- [ ]
- [ ]
- [ ]
- [ ]
- [ ]

Notes

_____
_____
_____

Weekly Clean

Monday

Tuesday

Wednesday

Thursday

Friday

Saturday & Sunday

Notes

Weekly Clean

Monday

Tuesday

Wednesday

Thursday

Friday

Saturday & Sunday

Notes

Weekly Clean

Monday
- [ ]
- [ ]
- [ ]
- [ ]
- [ ]
- [ ]

Tuesday
- [ ]
- [ ]
- [ ]
- [ ]
- [ ]
- [ ]

Wednesday
- [ ]
- [ ]
- [ ]
- [ ]
- [ ]
- [ ]

Thursday
- [ ]
- [ ]
- [ ]
- [ ]
- [ ]
- [ ]

Friday
- [ ]
- [ ]
- [ ]
- [ ]
- [ ]
- [ ]

Saturday & Sunday
- [ ]
- [ ]
- [ ]
- [ ]
- [ ]
- [ ]

Notes

_____

_____

_____

Weekly Clean

Monday

Tuesday

Wednesday

Thursday

Friday

Saturday & Sunday

Notes

Weekly Clean

Monday

- [ ]
- [ ]
- [ ]
- [ ]
- [ ]
- [ ]

Tuesday

- [ ]
- [ ]
- [ ]
- [ ]
- [ ]
- [ ]

Wednesday

- [ ]
- [ ]
- [ ]
- [ ]
- [ ]
- [ ]

Thursday

- [ ]
- [ ]
- [ ]
- [ ]
- [ ]
- [ ]

Friday

- [ ]
- [ ]
- [ ]
- [ ]
- [ ]
- [ ]

Saturday & Sunday

- [ ]
- [ ]
- [ ]
- [ ]
- [ ]
- [ ]

Notes

_____

_____

_____

Weekly Clean

Monday

- [ ]
- [ ]
- [ ]
- [ ]
- [ ]
- [ ]

Tuesday

- [ ]
- [ ]
- [ ]
- [ ]
- [ ]
- [ ]

Wednesday

- [ ]
- [ ]
- [ ]
- [ ]
- [ ]
- [ ]

Thursday

- [ ]
- [ ]
- [ ]
- [ ]
- [ ]
- [ ]

Friday

- [ ]
- [ ]
- [ ]
- [ ]
- [ ]
- [ ]

Saturday & Sunday

- [ ]
- [ ]
- [ ]
- [ ]
- [ ]
- [ ]

Notes

_____
_____
_____
_____

Weekly Clean

Monday

Tuesday

Wednesday

Thursday

Friday

Saturday & Sunday

Notes

Weekly Clean

Monday
Tuesday
Wednesday
Thursday
Friday
Saturday & Sunday

Notes

Weekly Clean

Monday

Tuesday

Wednesday

Thursday

Friday

Saturday & Sunday

Notes

Weekly Clean

Monday

Tuesday

Wednesday

Thursday

Friday

Saturday & Sunday

Notes

Weekly Clean

Monday

Tuesday

Wednesday

Thursday

Friday

Saturday & Sunday

Notes

Weekly Clean

Monday

Tuesday

Wednesday

Thursday

Friday

Saturday & Sunday

Notes

Weekly Clean

Monday

Tuesday

Wednesday

Thursday

Friday

Saturday & Sunday

Notes

Weekly Clean

Monday
- [ ]
- [ ]
- [ ]
- [ ]
- [ ]
- [ ]

Tuesday
- [ ]
- [ ]
- [ ]
- [ ]
- [ ]
- [ ]

Wednesday
- [ ]
- [ ]
- [ ]
- [ ]
- [ ]
- [ ]

Thursday
- [ ]
- [ ]
- [ ]
- [ ]
- [ ]
- [ ]

Friday
- [ ]
- [ ]
- [ ]
- [ ]
- [ ]
- [ ]

Saturday & Sunday
- [ ]
- [ ]
- [ ]
- [ ]
- [ ]
- [ ]

Notes
_____
_____
_____
_____

Weekly Clean

Monday
Tuesday
Wednesday
Thursday
Friday
Saturday & Sunday

Notes

Weekly Clean

Monday

- [ ]
- [ ]
- [ ]
- [ ]
- [ ]
- [ ]

Tuesday

- [ ]
- [ ]
- [ ]
- [ ]
- [ ]
- [ ]

Wednesday

- [ ]
- [ ]
- [ ]
- [ ]
- [ ]
- [ ]

Thursday

- [ ]
- [ ]
- [ ]
- [ ]
- [ ]
- [ ]

Friday

- [ ]
- [ ]
- [ ]
- [ ]
- [ ]
- [ ]

Saturday & Sunday

- [ ]
- [ ]
- [ ]
- [ ]
- [ ]
- [ ]

Notes

Weekly Clean

Monday

- [ ]
- [ ]
- [ ]
- [ ]
- [ ]
- [ ]

Tuesday

- [ ]
- [ ]
- [ ]
- [ ]
- [ ]
- [ ]

Wednesday

- [ ]
- [ ]
- [ ]
- [ ]
- [ ]
- [ ]

Thursday

- [ ]
- [ ]
- [ ]
- [ ]
- [ ]
- [ ]

Friday

- [ ]
- [ ]
- [ ]
- [ ]
- [ ]
- [ ]

Saturday & Sunday

- [ ]
- [ ]
- [ ]
- [ ]
- [ ]
- [ ]

Notes

Weekly Clean

Monday

Tuesday

Wednesday

Thursday

Friday

Saturday & Sunday

Notes

Weekly Clean

Monday

Tuesday

Wednesday

Thursday

Friday

Saturday & Sunday

Notes

Weekly Clean

Monday

- [ ]
- [ ]
- [ ]
- [ ]
- [ ]
- [ ]

Tuesday

- [ ]
- [ ]
- [ ]
- [ ]
- [ ]
- [ ]

Wednesday

- [ ]
- [ ]
- [ ]
- [ ]
- [ ]
- [ ]

Thursday

- [ ]
- [ ]
- [ ]
- [ ]
- [ ]
- [ ]

Friday

- [ ]
- [ ]
- [ ]
- [ ]
- [ ]
- [ ]

Saturday & Sunday

- [ ]
- [ ]
- [ ]
- [ ]
- [ ]
- [ ]

Notes

Weekly Clean

Monday
- [ ]
- [ ]
- [ ]
- [ ]
- [ ]
- [ ]

Tuesday
- [ ]
- [ ]
- [ ]
- [ ]
- [ ]
- [ ]

Wednesday
- [ ]
- [ ]
- [ ]
- [ ]
- [ ]
- [ ]

Thursday
- [ ]
- [ ]
- [ ]
- [ ]
- [ ]
- [ ]

Friday
- [ ]
- [ ]
- [ ]
- [ ]
- [ ]
- [ ]

Saturday & Sunday
- [ ]
- [ ]
- [ ]
- [ ]
- [ ]
- [ ]

Notes
_____
_____
_____

Weekly Clean

Monday

Tuesday

Wednesday

Thursday

Friday

Saturday & Sunday

Notes

Weekly Clean

Monday
- [ ]
- [ ]
- [ ]
- [ ]
- [ ]
- [ ]

Tuesday
- [ ]
- [ ]
- [ ]
- [ ]
- [ ]
- [ ]

Wednesday
- [ ]
- [ ]
- [ ]
- [ ]
- [ ]
- [ ]

Thursday
- [ ]
- [ ]
- [ ]
- [ ]
- [ ]
- [ ]

Friday
- [ ]
- [ ]
- [ ]
- [ ]
- [ ]
- [ ]

Saturday & Sunday
- [ ]
- [ ]
- [ ]
- [ ]
- [ ]
- [ ]

Notes
_____
_____
_____
_____

www.ingramcontent.com/pod-product-compliance
Lightning Source LLC
Chambersburg PA
CBHW071316080526
44587CB00018B/3247